INVESTING HOW TO INVEST FOR BEGINNERS

Learn to generate wealth in your sleep and grow your money for the future

TABLE OF CONTENTS

CHAPTER ONE:
WHAT IS INVESTMENT

When you ask the ☐uestion what is investment, we can say it is putting your spare money to work for you. The way most of us were taught to make an income is to get a job and work a set amount of hours every week. The only problem is if you want more money you must work more hours at your job. That could mean giving up those leisure activities at the weekend so the extra money is of no use if you haven't got the time to spend it.

So if you want that free time to enjoy the money you must put your funds to work in a good investment. With investment you can be sleeping or performing, any other activity while still earning money. That is the true beauty of investing, you can really maximise your earnings potential. It won't matter if you don't work that overtime, you can still be making that extra money.

The most important concept for you to understand is the simple idea of putting your money to work for you. There are many investment vehicles available for you to invest in including mutual funds, stocks and shares, bonds, real estate or even starting up a business. Each of these investment vehicles has positives and negatives and you must be aware of those. Losing trades is part of the game so you must ride out the storm and hang around for those profits to come in.

Lets understand that investing is different from gambling. With gambling you are betting on an uncertain outcome in the hope you might win your bet. Or for example you get a hot tip from a friend at the bar, then this would be gambling as you did not analyse the market beforehand. You simply took a random stock pick from a friend. Real investors do not operate in this manner. A good investor will not just throw money at a random stock, instead he will carefully analyse things and put money in when there is a good chance of seeing a return on the investment.

So why do people even bother with investing? Well we all want to be able to afford more of the things we like in life. Most people also seek the freedom investing can bring. But in this day and age, gone are the days of being able to retire on a big fat pension. Governments are tightening their belts therefore the responsibility for having a good pension relies on you. So its best to have a sound plan in place to ensure you are financially stable in those later years.

FURTHER EXPLANATION ON INVESTMENT

The term investment is a very broad term and may not be easily comprehend just like any other subject. Investments also do not have a definite definition because people use it at different levels and on different situations. How warren buffet, the richest investor in the American stock market will define investment will be different from how a man on the street will define it.

Investment is the commitment of money or capital to purchase financial instruments or other assets in order to gain profitable returns in form of interest, income, or appreciation of the instrument.

Many people knew of the 80/20 rule also known as the principle of least efforts originated by the Italian economist Vilfredo Pareto in 1897. The rule says 80% of our success comes from 20% of our efforts. This rule is very real but not so real in the world of money and investment.

In the world of investment it's 90/10 rule. In other words, 10% of people make 90% of the money. In the world of movies, 10% of actors make 90% of the money. Also in the world of athletes, 90% of the money is made by 10% of the people, and same applies to the world of musicians.

This is to say that most people that say or think they are investors are only gamblers or speculators. All they do is invest due to a hot tip by maybe a financial magazine or from a radio presenter. It is called buy, hold, and pray. This is why we often hear of so many high income people such as lawyers, doctors, rock stars, and professional athletes losing money in less-than sound investments.

They have the money alright, but they lack the sophistication of investing. In other words, they have the money but don't know how to invest it safely and for high returns. All they see is deals that looks the same to them but they can't differentiate between a good investment and a bad one. It's advisable for such people to hire a professional money manager they trust to invest on their behalf.

According to Robert T. Kiyosaki, author of Rich Dad Poor Dad, to become a good investor or to really understand investment, one has to possess what he termed as the three "3-Es".

The "3-Es" are:

1. Education

2. Experience

3. Excessive cash

For you to have the above three, you have to pay a price, and the price is time. Yes, it takes time to be educated, it takes time to have experience and to have excessive cash except through inheritance.

However, in any field you choose to invest your money, it may be in stocks, bonds, mutual funds, insurance, commodities, collectibles, precious metal, real estate, etc, always remember that there will always be ups and downs and like gambling, investing can be a very emotional roller-coaster ride.

So when you invest, know where the market is going, and focus on reaching your final target. Don't get flustered when you see major fluctuations in the market. Investing can be very emotional and sometimes entertaining. Just buckle up and enjoy the ride.

CHAPTER TWO:
TYPES OF INVESTMENT

A stock market is also known as an e□uity market. A stock market is an open market for the trading of company-owned stock as well as their plagiaristic at a consented price. You must have heard that markets are never still. Markets are always moving - effecting forever changing scenarios. This is the sole reason why the stock market is said to be unstable. It is very complicated or to a certain extent not viable to predict the market precisely. Sometimes it just booms and along with it the economy raises and at other times, bang, it just collapses. There is no warning for the investors. Whenever there is a boom in the market, people like to call it a bull run in the stock And when it is falling, people call it a bear run happening in the market. It is very important to know the different types of investment. There are basically 3 types.

About the stock market

The stock market makes available a really first-class likelihood for stock investors to swiftly make money as well as grow their made money. There is practically no better way around to making such easy money! But at the same time, the market is also very capricious and also very risky.

There are three types of investments:

Low risk

High risk

Moderate risk

Low risk investments

Low risk investments the investments that have more stability, but with a lower ROI or low return on investment. At the same time, they are more predictable

High risk investments

High risk investments do typically give back a much higher rate of return on investment or ROI, but at the same time, they are more inclined to experience severe highs and excessive lows. This results in an increased likelihood of loss. They are much less predictable than low risk investments in the share market.

Here is the no-win situation: any particular investment cannot be segregated as a purely high-risk or a purely low risk investment. But never panic!

Moderate risk investments

The moderate risk investments are typically those that give back a higher rate of return on investment or ROI than lower risk in investments but a comparatively lower rate of return on investment or ROI than higher risk in investments. At the same time, they are more inclined to experience more highs and lows as compared to lower risk and lesser fluctuations compared to high risk. Similarly, they are less predictable than low risk investments but more so than high risk investments.

So how do we get the best ones?

Do the following:

1. Even out the chief companies.

2. Revise their stock market descriptions.

3. Center a large amount of your concentration to parties that have the overriding credentials of stock market prize money - there is a lot of such business out there!

4. Also be on the look out for the silent ones. Some of them may not have come under the public eye but have been doing rather well for themselves in the market. Capitalize on such opportunities if you happen to come across some!

5. Participate in it out of harm's way. You call for to never be antagonistic in the stock market. Being belligerent possibly will bestow on you gigantic increases upon an episode of time, but at one fell swoop, they in addition transport within immense hazards! As a result have fortitude and participate in it in safe hands. Your income may not be something to blow your own horn about but it will at any rate be unshakable and you will have that all important gain in the haggle - self-possession.

STOCK MARKET INVESTING

Stock market is subjected to fre☐uent changes. Uncertainties are ☐uite frequent in this area and hence investors who are people involved in this business must be extremely cautious. But still then stock investment is a way of making easy profit as compared to real estate and bond investment. If you are planning or have already planned to invest in the susceptible and speculative stocks market, then, you should get concerned about using an effective investment program that'd help you to make right investments in appropriate time. With thousands of stocks listed in the stocks market, it becomes very difficult to make a correct immediate decision, and therefore a right working automated stock program can turn out to be at real advantage for you. However, selecting a good stock program will help you to make informed decisions in the manner such that you register phenomenal increase in the value of your investments. Here are the ways which will help you in selecting an effective automated stocks investment program:

1. Money Back Guarantee- Choose the stock program that comes with money back guarantee. If you are not getting the money back guarantee on the stock program, then it

should immediately set the warning signals that there's absolutely something fishy and wrong. A money back guarantee will allow the investor to test the stock investment program in real time scenario. The program will measure the performances of few stocks picks in the market and gives the investor information on the stocks. Make sure that you do not take a step forward in taking this type of automated program. With a valid money back guarantee option, the investor can have the legitimate way to analyze and invest in the stocks market

2. The stock investment program that you go with should be designed for penny stocks, which requires completely different analytical process. Penny stocks are the fast way of doubling or even tripling your investments in the stock trading. It is ☐uite remarkable to see that if an investor can predict the market behavior of the penny stock ☐uite early before it follows the market trends, it is very likely that an investor makes good amount of money. But, all this can only happen, if the investor makes the right choice when selecting stock investment program.

3. Stock investment program should be user-friendly by its very nature. An investor who is new or who has little idea about the investments in the stocks should be able to make the investments by using stock investment program. Therefore, the ease of use of the automated program will give the investor an upper edge when he or she makes the investments in the stocks.

4. Make sure that the stock investment program is effective in doing the technical analysis, as this is essential for make right judgments when investing in stocks. The automated program should give an investor the advantage of making the investments by following correct technical analysis.

5. The stock investment program that you purchase should be affordable and not over prices for any reason. If the automated stock investment program is over valued, it is very likely that you have to pay more from your pocket than what you eventually earn from the investments in the stocks.

Follow these points with extreme seriousness when you go for choosing stock investment program for increasing the prospects from your investments.

REAL ESTATE

Real estate investing involves ac□uisition, holding, and sale of rights in real property with the expectation of using cash inflows for potential future cash outflows and thereby generating a favorable rate of return on that investment.

More advantageous than stock investments (which usually require more investor equity) real estate investments offer the advantage to leverage a real estate property heavily. In other words, with an investment in real estate, you can use other people's money to magnify your rate of return and control a much larger investment than would be possible otherwise. Moreover, with rental property, you can virtually use other people's money to pay off your loan.

But aside from leverage, real estate investing provides other benefits to investors such as yields from annual after-tax cash flows, e□uity buildup through appreciation of the asset, and cash flow after tax upon sale. Plus, non-monetary returns such as pride of ownership, the security that you control ownership, and portfolio diversification.

Of course, capital is required, there are risks associated with investing in real estate, and real estate investment property can be management-intensive. Nonetheless, real estate investing is a source of wealth, and that should be enough motivation for us to want to get better at it

Real estate is not purchased, held, or sold on emotion. Real estate investing is not a love affair; it's about a return on investment. As such, prudent real estate investors always consider these four basic elements of return to determine the potential benefits of purchasing, holding on to, or selling an income property investment.

1. Cash Flow - The amount of money that comes in from rents and other income less what goes out for operating expenses and debt service (loan payment) determines a property's cash flow. Furthermore, real estate investing is all about the investment property's cash flow. You're purchasing a rental property's income stream, so be sure that the numbers you rely on later to calculate cash flow are truthful and correct.

2. Appreciation - This is the growth in value of a property over time, or future selling price minus original purchase price. The fundamental truth to understand about appreciation, however, is that real estate investors buy the income stream of investment property. It stands to reason, therefore, that the more income you can sell, the more you can expect your property to be worth. In other words, make a determination about the likelihood of an increase in income and throw it into your decision-making.

3. Loan Amortization - This means a periodic reduction of the loan over time leading to increased e□uity. Because lenders evaluate rental property based on income stream, when buying multifamily property, present lenders with clear and concise cash flow reports. Properties with income and expenses represented accurately to the lender increase the chances the investor will obtain a favorable financing.

4. Tax Shelter - This signifies a legal way to use real estate investment property to reduce annual or ultimate income taxes. No one-size-fits-all, though, and the prudent real estate investor should check with a tax expert to be sure what the current tax laws are for the investor in any particular year.

REAL ESTATE MARKETING TOOLS

1. A Real Estate Website

Each day in your market area, hundreds (possibly thousands) of home buyers and sellers turn to the Internet for real estate information. Having a real estate website is the first step to connecting with this ideal audience. Thus, the website is a core marketing tool for real estate in the modern age.

2. A Web "Presence"

What's the difference between a web presence and a website? Plenty. A website is a grain of sand on a long beach, with little hope of standing out in any significant way. But a web presence increases the chance people will find you online. A web presence includes such things as the real estate website, online press releases, real estate blogging and other online ventures. your chances of be. In an age where so many people use the Internet for real estate research, a strong web presence is a necessary marketing tool for real estate success.

3. A Real Estate Blog

In my opinion, real estate blogs can be one of the most effective marketing tools for real estate agents. Especially when they're used properly. When you publish □uality content to a real estate blog on a regular basis, you are increasing your web presence (mentioned above). You're also positioning yourself as an authority in your area. These are just a few of the reasons a blog makes a good marketing tool for real estate success.

4. Client Referrals

It's no secret that client referrals lead to a lot of business in the real estate industry. So in this regard, referrals are a powerful marketing tool for real estate agents. But some agents forget that the process leading up to a good referral begins on Day 1 of the working relationship. Take good care of your clients from first contact to closing day, and you'll tap into one of the most powerful marketing tools for real estate -- the client referral.

5. A Modern Outlook

The Internet has forever changed real estate research, as well as the real estate transactions themselves. So it's important for real estate agents to adopt a modern way of thinking about their business. Start with what consumers are doing today, how they're using the Internet, etc. Work backwards from there? How can you use that to your advantage? Keep a modern outlook toward real estate, and you'll ac□uire yet another marketing tool for real estate success.

BOND INVESTING

Bond investing is the safest way to invest long term. One of the safest ways to invest is in bonds. If you are thinking about investing in bonds, chances are you are making a very good decision. You should be able to make a little bit of money on your investments - and you are not very likely to lose any money in the deal. However, while the stock market is confusing, the bond market is too. Therefore, before you start investing in the bond market, you should do some research and make sure you can find out what you need to know about bonds.

Bond investing is one way for investors to receive a regular fixed income, and it is a particularly popular form of investment during shaky times in the stock market. That is because bonds typically offer less volatility than stocks, although that is not to say that the bond market does not have uni☐ue risks of its own.

A bond is basically a loan from you to a government or company. That government or company uses the bond as a way to borrow money in return for paying it back with a certain amount of interest over a certain amount of time. That period of time can range from months to decades. Has a relative ever given you a savings bond? That is one form of bond. In that case, the federal government is the borrower.

Federal bonds are some of the safest investments available. Because of this, the interest rate is lower compared to most other bonds. However, the risk of the federal government not paying you back is minuscule compared to just about any other potential borrower.

Municipal bonds are offered by local governments such as cities, counties, or states, these local governments sometimes feel the need to take on bond debt in order to finance special projects that they otherwise would be unable to afford at the time. As a bonus, municipal bond holders often are exempt from paying taxes on the interest income they receive.

Corporate bonds are offered by many of the same companies that are listed on stock markets. Since stock offerings are a one-time way for companies to raise funds, companies use corporate bonds in much the same way that governments use bonds-for the funding of something special that wouldn't be affordable at the time without outside help from people involved in bond investing.

It is important for bond investors to be aware of the risks and rewards of bonds. Not all borrowers are e☐ual. Standard & Poor's and Moody's are the two major services out there to help you evaluate the creditworthiness of potential borrowers. The safest investments are with borrowers rated with an A or with multiple A's. Those with low grades, often called junk bonds, run a much higher risk of defaulting on their loans. However, people have been known to get rich from investing in junk bonds-just make sure any money you invest in that area is money you could afford to lose.

As is the case with any investment, it is important for investors to carefully assess their current investment situations and goals for the future. If you are looking for an investment that offers regular interest income, are looking to hedge against downturns in other markets, or you simply want to keep your portfolio diverse, bond investing may be the right fit for you.

CHAPTER THREE:

INVESTMENT TIPS - WHY YOU SHOULD INVEST IN SOMETHING YOU KNOW ABOUT

One of the best investment tips you could ever learn is to invest in the things that you know about. There are plenty of new businesses that come out with ideas that have not been explored yet, but the problem with investing in them is that you probably have no experience with whatever it is they are promoting. Certainly, you can make money investing in something you have no knowledge of whatsoever, but your odds of doing so are greatly reduced this way. Here are a few reasons why you may want to invest in a niche you are familiar with.

The reason investing in familiar territory is one of the best investment tips out there is because you can make much better decisions for your money when you know about a business. This gives you an idea of who your audience is, where your target market lies, and possibly where you should put your biggest financial efforts. The more you know, the easier it is to make those tough choices that could change your business for better or worse. You can avoid those awkward moment that could be bypassed with experience.

Other investment tips are plenty valid to look into, but you should fully grasp this idea before you spend any money on a project you know nothing about. If you are going into a joint venture, being familiar with whatever you are investing in will prevent you from being scammed by the others in the investment. While this may be unpleasant to think about, you need to be prepared for problems like that. You can remain knowledgeable enough to protect your money if you go in knowing something about it in the first place.

This is one of the investment tips that will save you time as well because you will not have to fumble around with research from the start. While it is always a good idea to spend time researching about a new business adventure you have, knowing about a niche will spare you a lot of time learning the basics. You may enjoy your investment more if you know about it as well, and your passion for the matter may inspire other people to take notice as well. If you keep your energy up about a certain topic, you should be able to get a good profit from it in the end. Property investment can be a good way of investing for the future.

WHY PEOPLE INVEST IN PROPERTIES

Putting your money in the bank for safekeeping is a good idea, but it would be better if you use it for investing in a property that would become your lifetime asset. It has a more practical and advantageous use -- you can use it as your second residence or as a vacation home, rent it out for business, or sell it out later for profit.

Appreciation is one of the reasons why property is the perfect investment for many entrepreneurs. Despite the fact that market prices of homes around the globe are dropping due to the economic turmoil that hit many of big countries today, investors are still looking forward to achieve a long-term goal in turning a piece of property into a asset that they can profit from in the near future.

But these are not sufficient facts that explain why people invest in properties for stable financial future.

Passive Income - Earning After Retirement

Having your own property is a great way to earn passive income for the future. You're still earning a decent income even when you're retired from work. Despite the risk in the real estate business, many find it a convenience to own a profit for long-term goals. For example, if you own a residential property now and have no immediate use for it; you can turn it into a rental business later one for added income. This is perfect for those who are considering their financial status when they reach retirement.

Tax Benefits - Paying Less Tax Than Usual

Tax has always been a problem of many entrepreneurs today, but a property tax can be used to your advantage if you know the legal term that comes with it. You will get to pay less depending on the depreciation.

Taxes depreciate over the year and you can get good amount of savings from it. If you get to pay $3,000 worth of tax for this year, you get to pay less for the succeeding years depending on the percentage of the depreciation.

Profit For The Future - Capital Growth

Keep in mind that the real estate market has never been a stable venture. The market price of your home varies from time to time. It goes up and down without even a moment's notice. One advantage to this, however, is the fact that you still own the property -- whatever its price in the market.

In most cases, properties -- both commercial and residential -- increase its market value over time. You might have bought the property for $300,000 but there is a possibility of doubling the amount after a few years; giving you a good profit.

Million-Dollar Goal

Investing in properties can be a safe vehicle for you to earn millions of dollars in the future. Many, however, testified that being successful in the venture was never an easy feat; but those who are successful at it are bragging a lot of figures in their bank accounts.

If you're planning to earn a sizable income or profit from property investments then it is best to be careful and come prepared. Planning helps eliminate common factors that contribute to failure and pave way to a successful investment for a stable financial future.

CHAPTER FOUR:
HOW TO GET STARTED INVESTING

If you have some hard earned money and you want to make it work for you and give you a return, you will have one burning question How do I start investing?

There are many considerations that you will have to think about before this question can be answered. The financial investment options are innumerable and each one is dependent upon your particular circumstances. It is very easy to approach an expert and seek some advice. You cannot, however, just walk in to the office of a financial investment advisor with the ☐uestion how do I start investing? and expect a short and definitive answer. You should ask yourself some other ☐uestions first.

Do I have credit cards bills with outstanding sums which are costing interest of more than 10%? If so, then you may be wise to reduce these outstanding debts so that they are not costing you more than the interest that you will be earning on your investment. How long do I want tie up my money in an investment scheme? Some schemes, such as stocks, will be best entered into for a minimum of five years at least. If you are investing money for retirement or education, for example, make sure that you have considered the time scale. These are just a couple of thoughts to consider before you approach the how do I start investing ☐uestion.

One of the other great considerations is the risk that you are willing to take. As a general rule of thumb, the higher the risk, the greater the return. Sometimes obviously there will be an exception to this rule but this a thought to bear in mind.

The problem is that if you do not know about investing, it can be confusing. With so many different investment vehicles around, it is hard to choose which one to get involved in.

Although, there are many investment vehicles, you do not have to go overboard and invest in everything at the beginning. All you need to do is begin with one, two, or three investment types.

A word of warning: Make sure you have your bills taken care of before you start. This is because you will be taking a certain percentage of your money you make, and placing it in your investments. This is why you need to be as debt free as possible.

When you start investing, the best way to do it is to arrange for a percentage to come from your paycheck. You can set up your investments by either having money taken from your paycheck automatically, or just remember, when you get paid, and when you deposit your paycheck, to have the percentage you agreed to, taken out and applied to your accounts.

As for the type of investment, that will depend on what you want to invest in. If you want to invest in the long-term, you will want to look into investment that you can pay into and that will grow over time, with interest, if possible.

The investment you choose will determine what amount of money you will need. If you decide to go with stocks, they will usually be the preferred investment type. So when you get paid, you will go for that as the main investment vehicle.

Most people who start out with investing have no idea where to begin. Here are some apps that could be downloaded in your mobil phone's app store.

Acorns: Acorns is a free app can be downloaded easily and quickly. All that has to be done is link your banking card to the account, whenever you send money on the card, the spare change from purchases will be rounded up to the next dollar and invested into a portfolio. You can also set up a risk tolerance to lower your chance of going too over board. There is a small monthly fee for using the app which is up to 25% of your annual assets.

Robinhood: This app is specially targeted torward beginners to the investment field. Robinhood is a brokerage service that offers free trading. You also have to link a debit card or bank account in order to get stated with trading.

Betterment: Betterment is another app that helps investors with managing their spending habits, grow and protect their wealth, and save money. Fees range from 0.15 to 0.35 percent of your annual balance.

Before Investing and using the apps that have been listed above, also download an app called, *Invest: Learn how to invest in stocks*. This app guides you by the hand when it comes to learning how to invest. Slides are included that can be read, you can also select that the section has been read and completed and you move on to other parts of investing. Before you know it, you will be investing.

Taking leaps of fate is what is needed sometimes in life, and these apps help you save and invest without you even having to remember to.

THE PROS AND CONS OF INVESTING

These days it seems like everyone is worried about their financial stability, and whether their savings are safe and sound. In the past few years, many people have seen market changes and economic instability affect their savings accounts and retirement funds, and it can be very disheartening to learn that all of the money you worked so hard to put away is gone in an instant. Many people think of investing as a way to bulk up their financial portfolios and ensure some income in the future when they may not be working as much. It's important to realize that making an investment in the stock market is different than saving, but it can be a good idea when pursued cautiously.

Most people choose to define investing as a way to make money by spending your money. Another way to think about it is that it's a way to have your money working for you all the time, instead of merely sitting in an account somewhere earning small amounts of interest. The big difference between investments and savings accounts is that people who save are mostly concerned with protecting the amount of money that they started with. Investors are more interested in using that lump sum to earn significant returns on their money in a shorter amount of time.

There are a couple of important concepts to understand about investing, and they are ownership and risk. One of the most attractive ☐ualities of public investments is that the owners of the stock in a company are in effect part owners of the company itself. Just like the acting owners, these shareholders have the ability to vote on decisions that affect the whole company, and in some cases, share in the profits that the company achieves.

Risk is another important concept of investing, and it is the reason why it is always good to seek financial advice before you start to sink your money into investment.

The value of stocks and companies fluctuates regularly, though usually it is so small that it doesn't affect the total investment. In some cases, companies that seemed very promising end up going bankrupt after a few years, and the shareholders are left with worthless pieces of paper that used to represent their money. Understanding this risk will help you to research the companies that you're interested in and make sound decisions about who you trust with your money.

TOP

Thank you for purchasing this ebook!

Book 2 is coming soon

Please leave your honest review with a rating to help make the books better and stronger for the readers!

www.ingramcontent.com/pod-product-compliance
Lightning Source LLC
Chambersburg PA
CBHW070308190526
45169CB00004B/1544

* 9 7 8 1 5 3 0 3 8 1 1 5 9 *